Where's My Hat?

Activity Book

By Hannah Fish

Name: ______________________

Age: ______________________

Class: ______________________

School: ______________________

Activities for pages 2–3

1 Match.

1 Rosie

2 Ben

3 Grandpa

2 Find and write the words.

1 hello 2 ______

3 ______ 4 ______

Activities for pages 4–5

1 Look at the picture.
Draw and color Clunk.

Activities for pages 6–7

1 Put a tick (✓) or a cross (X) in the box.

1 This is Clunk. 

2 This is a jacket. ☐

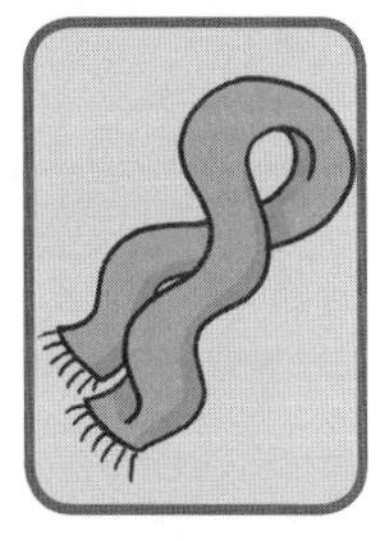

3 This is a hat. ☐

4 This is Ben. ☐

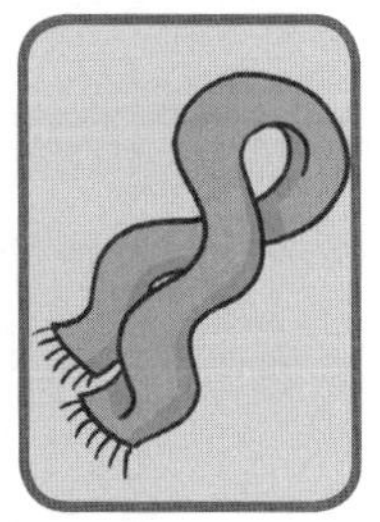

5 This is a scarf. ☐

2 Trace and write the words.

3 Circle *yes* or *no*.

1 Grandpa has a jacket. **yes** **no**

2 Grandpa has a black jacket. **yes** **no**

3 Grandpa has a brown jacket. **yes** **no**

4 Grandpa has a scarf. **yes** **no**

5 Clunk can see the scarf. **yes** **no**

Activities for pages 8–9

1 Match.

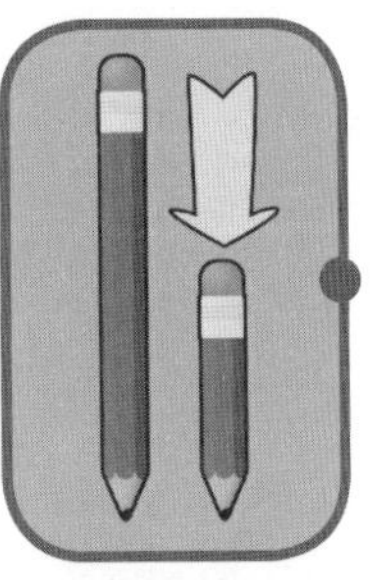

• 1 long

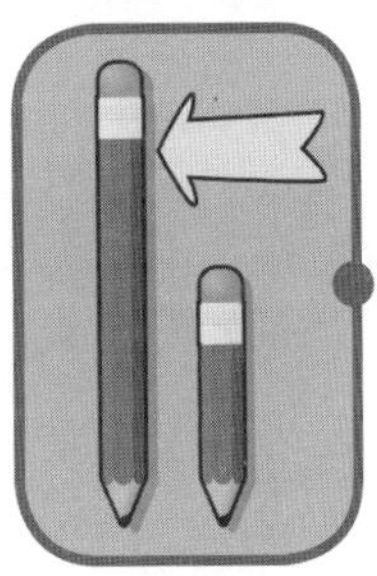

• 2 short

2 Circle the correct words.

1 Clunk is a …

2 Grandpa has a scarf. His scarf is …

long short

3 And his scarf is …

green red brown

3 Look at the picture. Put a tick (✓) or a cross (✗) in the box.

1 I can see Clunk. ☐

2 I can see Ben. ☐

3 I can see Grandpa. ☐

4 Grandpa has a scarf. ☐

5 Clunk has a jacket. ☐

Activities for pages 10–11

1 Match.

jacket Rosie hat Ben scarf

2 Put a tick (✓) or a cross (✗) in the box.

1 This is a door. ☐

2 This is a scarf. ☐

3 Circle *yes* or *no*.

1	Grandpa has a scarf.	**yes**	**no**
2	Grandpa has a green scarf.	**yes**	**no**
3	Clunk can see Grandpa's hat.	**yes**	**no**
4	Ben has a hat.	**yes**	**no**
5	Grandpa goes to the door.	**yes**	**no**

Activities for pages 12–13

1 Find the words.

t	h	G	b	e
C	e	r	u	n
l	a	a	c	f
u	d	n	h	d
n	l	d	b	o
k	f	p	c	o
e	h	a	t	r

2 Look at the picture. Draw and color the hats.

After-Reading Activities for pages 4–13

1 Write, draw, and color the Picture Dictionary.

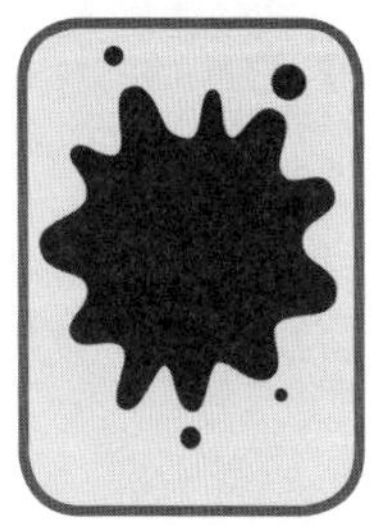

black

brown

____

green

____

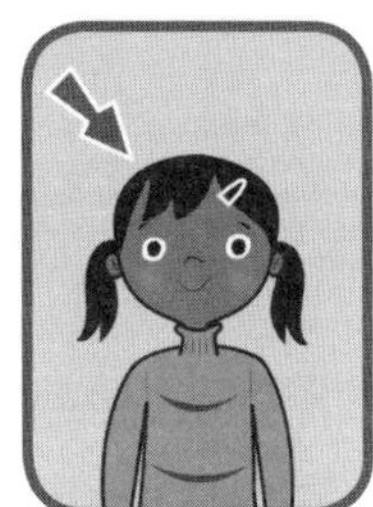

____

jacket

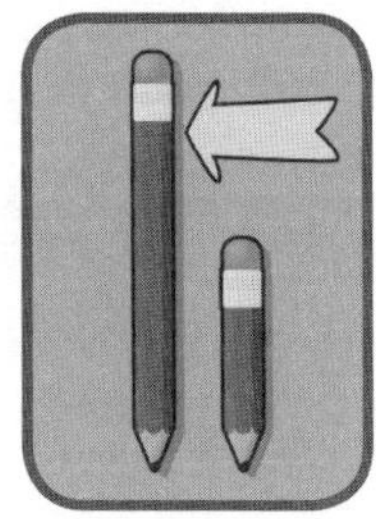

____

red

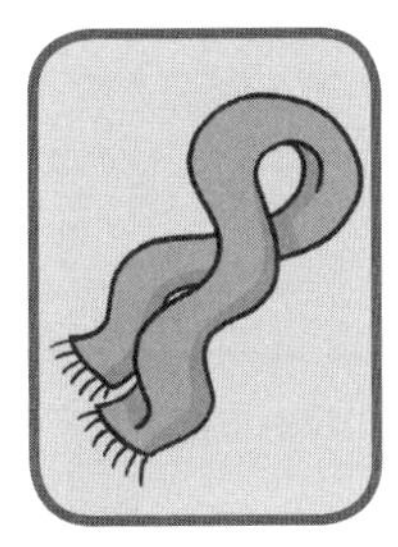

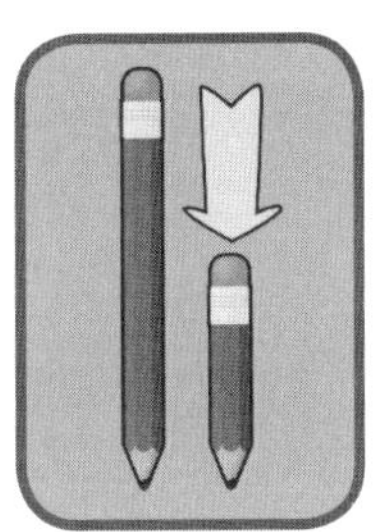

Draw and write your favorite word.

2 Complete the puzzle. Then write the secret word.

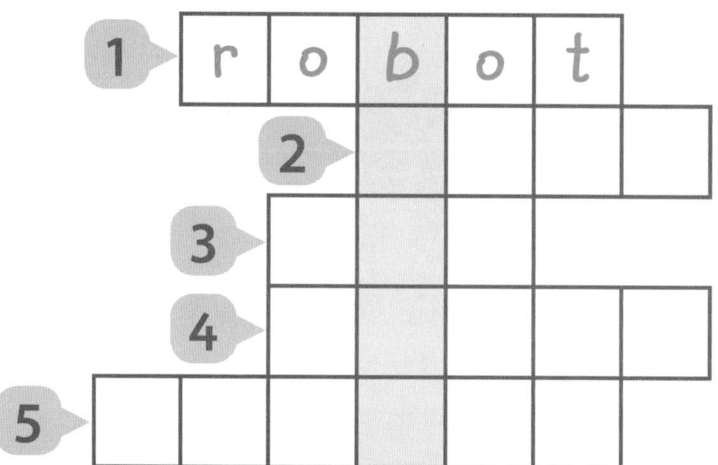

1

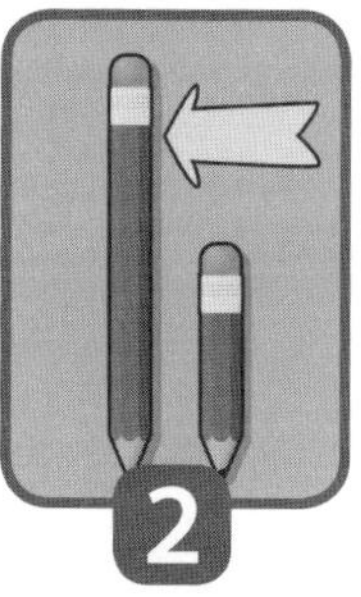
2

3

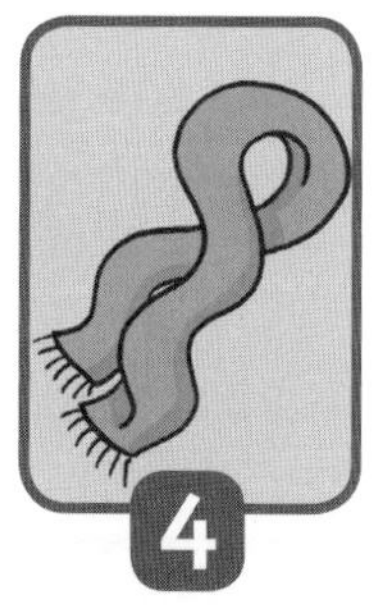
4

5

The secret word is b _ _ _ _

My Book Review

Draw and write your favorite character.

My favorite character is ______________.

What I like about this book

My favorite page is ______________.

My favorite picture is on page ______________.

Draw ☺, ☺☺, or ☺☺☺.

I like this book. 

I like the pictures. 

Great Clarendon Street, Oxford, OX2 6DP, United Kingdom

Oxford University Press is a department of the University of Oxford. It furthers the University's objective of excellence in research, scholarship, and education by publishing worldwide. Oxford is a registered trade mark of Oxford University Press in the UK and in certain other countries

First published in 2015

2024

10 9 8 7 6

ISBN: 978 0 19 472233 9

Printed in China

This book is printed on paper from certified and well-managed sources

ACKNOWLEDGEMENTS

Front cover illustration by: Steve Cox.

Additional illustrations by: Dusan Pavlic/Beehive illustration, Alan Rowe, Mark Ruffle.